CW00506320

headspun

written and illustrated by

mashnun munir

thank you amu, for giving me the space in this world to find my own
thank you nanu, for giving me the space the breathe

ধন্যবাদ আম্মু, আমাকে এই পৃথিবীতে নিজের জায়গা খুঁজে দেওয়ার জন্য
ধন্যবাদ নানু, আমাকে শ্বাস নেওয়ার জায়গা দেওয়ার জন্য

table of contents

table of contents

two

table of contents

three

headspun is about finding and building the blocks for a space greater than the one you're already existing in, and unraveling all of the things in that space that have been waiting patiently for your arrival. this space holds universes to discover, and we all begin our pilgrimage the moment we accept our calling. this is my pilgrimage, not guided by a compass or by the placement of the stars, but by the paranoia laced inside me simultaneously searching for its way out, told in phrases that i've been spending the entirety of my life learning how to say. the voyage towards self discovery is uncertain. it doesn't lead to light, but it does lead to peace.

my acumen for life is a product of low income communities, broken family ties, and a longing for faith clashing with ceaseless sins. spending countless days getting into trouble outside to avoid what's going on indoors, just to bring everything full circle. this is the voice of a penniless, deprived, yet hopeful brown skinned boy, caught in the crossfire of his environment, in hopes of finding prosperity.

to old friends, to my past life still sleeping through the trauma, to my wrongdoings which have kept me still, to my mother whose bond is far too wise for me to understand, to my father whom i have hopes of reconnecting with someday, and to the almighty, these phrases are given weight by the blocks handed over by you. after years of resentment and apprehension, i've finally found the power to let them out.

all praise to the most high

one

a muslim boy monologue

why do i echo prayers to ghosts in the midst of crisis
even though i feel my cries are lifeless
my mother tells me to stop crying because god is trying
my path to faith has been indecisive
even the imam has vices
before it was made a crime
war was just a way to survive
we're meant to be saved from our sins
what if i can't be saved from mine
it's hell on earth and we accept it
the man who sins the world
continues to live a life so precious
the homeless man who gives the world
is left in the streets breathless
why do we have to die to see heaven
is heaven a destination or just a state of mind
is heaven in this state of mine
is heaven in the room i end my day
when i kneel to the hard wood floor and pray
my grandmother tells me she's praying for me
i have demons preying on me
they live under my bed, masked as memories
serenading me the nights i fear them the most
i fear god and i fear death
my mother speaks of both so calmly
i've always dreamt of being closer to god
some nights i thought about speeding up the process
i wonder if these prayers will even do me any good
if my day of judgment will last an eternity
or if i will be understood

garment district

i weave together dreams of the garment district
but here i am
i'm unraveling each thread
everyone sees my loose ends
my family has me sewed
for i may seem stressed
hunger and agitation
poke nerves as would
needles through fabric

and if my faith
does not give me the power
to lace a soul together
i will be left
in stitches
just another shattered dream
of rags to riches

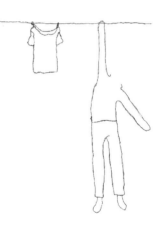

is this a home

ask me where i'm from
it's not a one word
answer

sober up
no toast
no blunt
silenced
deprived
brown skinned boys
don't rest
they antagonize the beauty of the dawn
they don't know where their voices have gone
no pretty pictures
i lost mine when i saw guns get drawn
my home rests when i enter my own
i don't open up
i haven't woken up

home is where the heart
grieves
jealous of the sky
after your plug says he's dry
after your very
very last
goodbye
so tell me
is this home
really a home for you
and i

screen door

we were poor
we've seen war
we don't speak on what we saw through a screen
we speak on what we've seen
through the screen door

don't put on your new black tee
i'd rather see you in bed tonight
it's dark past our porches
but we always stayed awake
to see more

lancaster

i walked up to lancaster
learned how to load a clip
learned survival
and survivors guilt
learned different points of views
i talk to
god
but he never wore my shoes
i've seen blood turn to paintings on concrete
some stains don't wash away
watching feens get a fix a block away
breath desperate for space to exist within
cracking bottles into knives
in the blink
of an eye
these are tears to cry
this is flying on standby
waiting

what has been seen cannot ever be
unseen
unforeseen
expected to last forever
anywhere but near

until it has proven to be eternally
seen
foreseen
here

turns out alright

they called me a failure
but failure means having tried
i had holes in my pockets
pennies to deposit
dirty money in my closet
disparity like little boys having to man homes
nowhere to hide
mother gave me 20 for eid and i flipped it
that's all she had
that all we had
why is god so patient with his saviors
yet so agile with his torment

i couldn't find an epiphany
so an epiphany found me
in a run down community in orlando
with gravel as graves
with credence to pave
disparity like little boys seeking shelter in playgrounds
looking for a way home
the weary turn a blind eye to success
hope is for the privileged
faith isn't concrete
my hoods concrete knows why i haven't tried
my hoods concrete tells no lies
and it knows my homes divide
but it houses the blocks to what i see inside
to what i keep inside
i smoke clouds darker than the ones above
soon we
will rise

the things we burn

i feel like the anger inside of our parents
broke down and reworked itself
into the fire
that is in these bodies of ours
heat consumes these bodies for hours
we know this heat very well
it's safe to say these homes were hell
and when you throw two young men in hell
the spirits and entities will speak for themselves
they will speak loud
and reckless and free
wishing their soliloquies were in tune

why do i feel like the smallest man in the room
but the closest to god
maybe because i'm always high
maybe because i'm always burning
maybe because the tears i cry
bring me to my knees
then through the cracks of these broken streets
then to the sky
then to god
then back
into this fire burning inside of me

between

i used to climb trees to the highest degree
and jump
to feel the
euphoria
connection
link
between mind and body
to soil and ground

grounded
a painful remedy from what's in the air
too dense to allow into my organs
treated as martyrs
weapons of mass
enlightenment

and then i climb back up
eager to jump
to feel at one with what's planted
with all those buried i eternally take for granted
i fear the rise more than the fall
becoming sediment

god gifted

snapbacks over fitteds
i think about all of the sins i've committed
profited off the contraband hidden under my bed
far from breath
i had a threesome with karma and death
in that bedroom
you'll find plenty bodies
somebody stop me

if my stories bring them chills
imagine how they make me feel
so many past lives i've lived
for me to live in the present
all these phrases wrapped in my head
so many more to open up
i'm still surprised with my gift
and i haven't even peaked

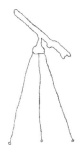

the hustle

i am god
who are you
look at you, trying to ignore me
trying to ignore me even though you are hungry
your stomach is singing
your mother is tired
screams don't fill empty mouths
nor empty souls
closed mouths don't get fed
they keep the most secrets
i am no secret, but a way of life
i give poor boys like you
bricks to build something of themselves
you are broke and you are broken
you are young and your skin is tainted
the hustle is already inside of you
how hunger and the hustle are so acquainted
what did you eat for dinner
that you did not repress
i know your lack of rest makes your vision blurry
don't worry
what the police thinks
or what your mother thinks
when you're found on the ground
clawing at the your hood's gravel for another dollar
everyone will understand as long as you trust me
you're not falling
that you are simply following your calling
that you are merely following god
even your mother said to never lose faith

two

what is lost in the trees is found in the soil

i still hear the ocean
i still hear the sirens
sometimes feeling numb
is just the mercy of god

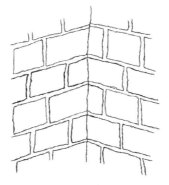

keep my name in vain

i told god to stop believing me
i told the bus driver to stop leaving me
i told myself to stop running
i wished for guidance
not for ink this black
not for skin to crack
not to sell another pack
i dip my arms into a pool of my past
and slowly watch the sorrow fill my sleeves
a final lullaby to my impatience and to what i believe
my coroner knows your name
incase my battling thoughts of righteousness and disgrace
meet halfway

mortal man

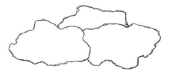

every chord played for burials
all sunday spent
each arpeggio a convocation for the dead
with every key
another door open
for us to be led
for words to be left unsaid

what is it that's keeping me alive

the little i have learned

i know i am destined for greatness
i know i am alive
because of my mother's whispers
from bedroom to night sky
5 times a day
i know my mother's garden grows not from light
but from the hope that
ran out the house over the years
a hope that she kneels for the earth to transcend
i know the earth was mended from dust
and to dust is where it shall return
i know my quran is buried in dust
i know my burial will be full of life
life from within that i'll carry from home to heaven
i know i'm from broken homes
that's maybe why i broke in homes
just to have money to eat
i know my sister tries teaching me about money and credit
while i'm trying to give myself enough credit to live
i know life is fragile like grand piano keys
my voice may not be heard in this life
but it will in the next
clear enough for every generation before me
to vibrate in its frequency
i know my ancestors are in the skies
hidden as ominous clouds
eager to cheer in rain
and clap in happy thunder
at the little i have learned
in the universe that is to discover

the afterlife

there's nothing sacred about war wounds
but still the war resumes
i kneel for prayer or i kneel towards collapse
all in hopes for more perhaps
the afterlife is meant to be a place of digression
but what to do with all these questions

oranges blossom

every voyage i've ever set foot on
turned itself into a journey
i cherish these corners
these hoods
these streets full of life
that crumble into memories
sneaking into my daydreams
into these brick walls
i feel like i've conquered the outside world
but i've yet to discover what's inside me
and who knows
if the old men
who ask for lighters on south street
carry the universe
in the bag on their shoulders
if the darkness we see them as
is really a galaxy of all things to unveil
if they share their dinner
with birds
flying back and forth
on an endless voyage
if they ever find their way back home

last

i smoke the same trees
my ancestors were hung from
every breath filled with the prayers and hope
i know they spoke with their last

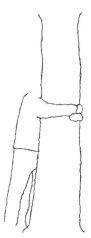

im coming home

i mask my intentions
in a silence that speaks phrases
with no translation

these phrases are not mine
they flow through me
gifted to me by something greater than you and i
shifting to a language
we understand

paradise

my mother finds my bottles and burn holes
as i find the words to tell her where i was
amu, memory prefers to house the explainable
grant me another night of forgiveness

three

funny stories

mother's limbs are brittle
so unlike the past she's
overcome
so unlike the scars she shows for fun
so unlike from where these poems come

now
she laughs in recollection of shattered dreams
survival becomes funny stories after maghrib
with whomever is left in this home
i listen softly
pain is tending to your mothers pain
her stories haunt me
i sin that same evening to maintain
i keep my secrets to keep her sane
how ungodly
i can't repay her in street credit
but i can with the dirty money i bring back home
how costly

her limbs grow tired of aching
so unlike the spirit she maintains
so unlike the resilience in her veins
her eyes breed hope
she rests
she remains

senseless

i am held by my mother's shattered arms
when it is my turn to mourn
lessons felt but unspoken
of how to open up
to trust in air
when you've grown a fear of breathing
every spirit from her soul has faced ends
she has planted her last seed in me
lifeless soil filled
with prayers that i am grander
than the story of a young man
who's imaginary friends found a way to disappear

senseless
i hear wood creaks at 2 am
of the nightly trek to her bedroom
she doesn't turn on the lights anymore

paranoia

as a child
i could not afford to dream
a prisoner in my own fantasy
i still pretend that i am asleep
i still embody pain
darker than the space
that holds the stars in the sky
but still the rules of the world apply
my lineage has spent too much time suffering
for me to be suffering with time
baba told me greed and stride
has sentenced him to life
i told him how much we are alike
these seeds were hand grown for us
bargaining price tags on ties to family
oh how reality parallels fantasy

at night
i sleepwalk with steps as soft as the clouds i hope to be
embodying the dreams that i know i'd be having
but only if they knew me

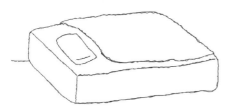

love poems

i want to be like those poets that write about love
about two lovers who ran away from home
through gardens and melodic sunsets
resting on a bed of roses
love ran away from my home in red agony
it turned to dust under my hoods streetlights
how beautiful, love
how precious, rest
i lay my shattered mother to rest when she grows tired of grieving
i hear her whispers for hope from her bedroom
she spent the day watering her garden
pleading for it to bride and blossom
i used to love writing
my pens have headaches
my bookmarks have stories
my journals have scars
a part of me ends when i think of a new poem
every phrase is a tear she could not weep
a night our havoc wouldn't let us fall asleep
poems about love are for people who think grief is temporary
when i transition
i hope my prayers and memories pass as well
just so i can spend my afterlife
reminiscing in sorrow release
singing with the sunset
resting on my bed of blossoming red roses
writing my little love poems in peace

when the family feuds

the soul
is split between
the childhood of the heart
and the aging of the mind
today i am finding prosperity
and placing it frontline
this duel seems endless
falling in the midst of our battleground
in hopes of calling a truce
and not remembering us at war

i throw my flag of pride across enemy lines
my forgiveness is not as easily defined
but i understand that emotions are mortal
that war crimes may be amnestied in the next life
that caskets are buried
with carnations deeply woven inside them
that there may be a place in heaven
for the angels we have murdered
that soldiers die honorably
with heartbeats in their hands
that bloodshed is imminent
when the family feuds

internal wars

he told me he was fighting an internal war
the kind you know you're going to lose
the kind where the opposition awakens your deepest fears
the kind that burns faith to ashes
the kind that makes you scared to look in the mirror
i've spent years beautifying his agony
an internal war that has laid so many like him
to rest
i used to wonder why he rested so much
maybe his dreams were the only worlds with sunsets
i try to join him at night
but his rests refuse my connection

my mother never rests until i'm back home
she fears i'll lose the internal war i've been fighting
ever since his transition

young boys who live in worlds like mine
know well of rest and war
how they intertwine
how they are closer than we may believe them to be
so close, that it can be difficult to tell them apart
so close, that the part in between the two,
presence,
may never even be felt

transition

some transition slowly, some just vanish
in the blink of an eye
the faithful travel to where they feel whole
but what about the darkness
what happens to the soul

my lifetime is timed
but this time is not mine
this poem is not mine
this blood is not mine
why god did you have to make us bleed
my father left and i've been lost ever since
i don't want to live on this island anymore
i'm with the homies getting high
watching smoke rise
transitioning so elegantly in its demise
i carry the burden of generational trauma in my eyes
desperate to find my epiphanies
i dream of treating past choices differently
i need forgiveness
forgiveness from being ungrateful for my blessings
forgiveness from coming home unconscious
forgiveness from letting him go
does suffrage lead to peace or just mask itself as lessons
i'm sick of learning
why can't peace be my lesson
may peace be upon us
my fear in living stems from losing the things i didn't know i needed
growing up and yearning for their presence

i need time to mourn

the proper space to grieve

i didn't realize until now
that when you say goodbye to someone you love
you have to say goodbye to them
for the rest of your life
when you aren't gifted the proper space to grieve
your chest becomes too empty to expand
desperate for room
you retrace each memory with trauma
and the new ones you make feel disconnected
when i create a new memory
i settle each one with a memorial
a parallel universe somewhere in my head
that one day will be laid to rest

i see you in everything
in the soil, in the rain
in these shattered walls when i'm in pain
it's hard to say goodbye to your own demons
they feed off the soil of your path towards hope
they grow stronger than any connection
you could make to your most vivid memories
i chase these memories
like hope
too far to ever really reach
but i'm still chasing
and i'll keep chasing
until our distant memories transition into new beginnings
ones that have proper endings
ones that don't require grievance
to reminisce

forgive me

when you make it through the fires
each step there on leaves the ground ablaze
the embers fade
but you can still feel it's heat,
it's presence
you can still feel it's spirit linger

i'll keep burning
until you transition me to ash
i'll keep breathing
until you gift me with my last

i'll be the fire for everything that has passed

اللَّهُمَّ اغْفِرْ لِي ذَنْبِي كُلَّهُ، دِقَّهُ وَجِلَّهُ، وَأَوَّلَهُ وَآخِرَهُ وَعَلَانِيَتَهُ وَسِرَّهُ

allaahum-maghfir lee thanbee kullahu, diqqahu wa jillahu, wa 'awwalahu wa 'aakhirahu wa 'alaaniyata hu wa sirrahu

o allah, forgive me for all my sins, great and small, the first and the last, those that are apparent and those that are hidden.
abu dawud: 878

Printed in Great Britain
by Amazon

17339736R00045